How The Bones May Fall

by
Roger Teas

Cadmus Publishing
www.cadmuspublishing.com

Copyright © 2022 Roger Teas

Published by Cadmus Publishing
www.cadmuspublishing.com
Port Angeles, WA

ISBN: 978-1-63751-147-3
Library of Congress Control Number: 2022900574

All rights reserved. Copyright under Berne Copyright Convention, Universal Copyright Convention, and Pan-American Copyright Convention. No part of this book may be reproduced, stored in a retrieval system, or transmitted in any form, or by any means, electronic, mechanical, photocopying, recording or otherwise, without prior permission of the author.

Contents

The Rest Can Be Burned 1
The Land of The Lost 2
What Creates This Science 3
To Design the Light 4
 Makes The Doubt Unhook 5
I Am Not an Expert 6
How Existence Is Retained 7
The Lonely Walk 9
What Is Faulted 10
It's Best Left Alone 11
Their Own Sort of Kingdom 12
Unblocking The Mind 13
And I Am Left Alone 14
How It Hurts to Pay this Price 15
The Means Is Just a Medium 17
 How A Tangle Is Undone 18
The Worst of Life's Distortions 19
Where My Focus Shall Remain 20
A Perplexing Mystery 21
I Admit That It Is Right 22
Of Its Own Mobility 23
Our Inevitable Questing 24
A Vast Indenture 25
What I've Let Myself Become 27
Misery Deplorable 28
My Integrity 29
I Am Also Horrified 30
This Long Unending Journey 31
The Sanctum of The Free 32
This I Call My Prayer 33
The Human Armory 34
The Discretion of My Deeds 35
All that I Am 36
That Abominable Sin 37

How The Bones May Fall 38
My Future on The Brink 39
To Clear My Mind 40
A Burdened World 41
A World Without Psychosis 42
As My Case Is Laid to Bed 43

HOW THE BONES MAY FALL

The Rest Can Be Burned

I do not believe in conspiracies in the usual idea.
I think they are misinterpreted in most of the media
The problem with understanding them lies in the portrayal
The intent of the creator of the story, or the fable.
It is impossible not to have strange event occur,
It is simply misconstrued as the word of mouth is stirred.
There is a long process of research to be done about it,
Before any conclusion becomes one plausibly founded
While other ideas are exaggerated far and outrageous.
Making for mainstream theories that are contagious.
A dissolution of the facts does a lot to protect
The mind from wandering into imagination unchecked
Their motives to consider in making a conclusion
What would be the purpose of their misinformations inclusion?
What does oneself great good to question the thought
The something averse or strange is in the plot.
I do not say cannot be true or not possible,
But that it is important to understand the obstacle.
That is placed before the viewer of a grand scheme
It may be that the perception is overwhelmed by the theme.
Of what may not even be such a spectacular cause,
I could just be out of range of the one taking pause.
With that in mind I don't put much in consideration,
If someone doesn't comprehend, they should not do litigation.
On any topic that could have multiple roots underground.
Or facts not related but ring to a similar sound.
Once there is a solid education that is earned,
The opinion that holds weight and the rest can be burned

The Land of The Lost

The pains of migraines attached to my head
Hot like a fire full of grief and mental stress
Thus began the day I was convicted in court
Reminiscent of accursed brought from hell's own sort
A lifelong nightmare with no break to awake
Left a question existence or what I did make
Is this the product of a diabolical nature?
If I have evil, then the world is now safer.
Yet, I cannot blame myself for what I am
I do not believe in evil, but creatures with different stands.
Something is strange in a world full of war
There are structural differences in each that is torn.
The mind inside of a person that is here,
Could have an origin of pain from a place of tears
There is no hate when the contrast is understood
There are spots of existence with no word for good
The sun burns hot with an atomic reaction
And scratches and hurts without regard to what happens
It has no compassion for those that don't survive.
And dictates the planet like a king with our lives
I am not in command and cannot know who is
As that entity is far too complicated and too big
With that I have no luxury to question my lot
Left to regulate myself to the land of the lost

What Creates This Science

I've always been curious about the forms of divination
Something about them have attracted my apt attention
I don't believe there are some types of find all answer
But that they are a link to another room unhampered
A connecting tool that brings one together with an entity
Human or not it is a being that exists from activity
Of its own kind and its own place that we don't see
In my eyes making it have its own right to then be
The same as us they may have many sorts of faults
Not exactly reliable to each question that is called
I have done much of a search into these beings
From having this opinion about these types of readings
I also don't have access to outside sources to do them
Leaving me on my own if I were ever to pursue them
I acknowledge the power of certain of these creatures
That have made bonds to people with divinatory features
There are to a great extent unfettered intelligences
That give access to their forms of what is meant and said.
These are of interest to me in a basic and simple sense
I wonder what they are and where they might make their nest
How they do exist in parallel to our own world
Is it separate or dependent or mixed together swirled?
In the end I will find out what creates this science
Most likely from its use and having faith and its reliance

TO DESIGN THE LIGHT

I've always thought that true talent is unattainable
That I have no worth I can call sustainable
I slowly began to realize that what talent is seen
Is not what is actually true talent to me
That what is in the visible and the known
Is an exploitation taking advantage of homes
A true talent does not have to be famous
It can be learned and done alone in basements
And the best ones are usually done like that
With no audience to scrutinize details and facts
To be liberated from any hate or opposition
And let loose in a realm of countless solutions
To not be fettered but any need or creed
Only the one that motivates your deed
It could be art or words are various knowledge
That becomes talent with unprecedented prowess
And still remains humble outside of the scrutiny
Of so many others that may cause a mutiny
To all of your work that has been developed
From the beginning of days that has propelled us
I am not to say that there cannot be a group
Of others that add fire or relate to your proof
The proof that knowledge and talent are one
That the poetic dance of each are equal in sum
That all else falls short in the age of art
And fame is only the result of the silent part
For alone in the dark in the time of night
The thoughts called of it to design the light

Makes The Doubt Unhook

I cannot name the cause of all the doubt
That feels the desire to search trees out
Every claim of each religion to unbearably different
From thoughts of atheism to buddha or the christians
Witchcraft and voodoo and the occult wisdom
At only more to the quest of this vision
Not only what lies beyond the veil of time
But what is inside us now with our thinking minds
The biggest question I have is simple and plain
Where's the end or start of material veins?
The universe itself sits in our realm of black
With too much possible to reliably attack
So, all the men made books in various subjects
Become a daunting task to decipher or bludgeon
As it will and does drive men insane
Looking for the truth like a desert for rain
And while I may find solace in each of the books
All of them together makes the doubt unhook

I Am Not an Expert

I understand what it means to be diagnosed mentally ill
But at the worst of times, I question my sanity still
There are things I think to write out or correlate
And decided not to as I am unsure of the sense it makes
My intention here is to relate what I go through
It sometimes my ideations are impossible to prove
It is a fear I have that I still be outcasts more
As if I am not already stigmatized to the core
I hope that I can find someone to help guide me
In the right and correct manner, I'm lost at finding
While I think at times, I may have some correct
I do not truly know as I am alone from the best
The kind of mind I need has to have knowledge
Of unusual things and schemes that are used as tutelage
To understand what encompasses their total truth
I am stuck in a position that does need such use
I at least need to prove I am capable to a degree
That I can be on my own when the direction is seen
I may not have a teacher or tutoring at the moment
And have still found a truth that can stand a showing
But it's like taking a test with no results to mark
Down how precise I have come to the spark
Of right mind and intelligence that does in fact create
Societies at large that each nation has done made
All I can hope for is feedback from these poems
As I am not an expert, and I don't profess to know them

How Existence Is Retained

Time is a conundrum I cannot seem to surpass
It is a sludge that barely moves as a mass
Of effects rolling and rippling through the clockwork
Only the dictation of the days can undo the murk
Of innumerable causations that occur in each day
Left at its mercy I have to play around its ways
The fruition that comes from one completed task
Makes the wait worthy of another to be had
These scenarios never end that again begin to start
One after another are extended far into the dark
Of an unseen law that never fails to bring forth
What we send into it with no other choice to court
We have but one option in this life that we're making
To bend our will through time creates unending patience
To end the monotonous waiting is actually far worse
As then the wait is for nothing at all of any worth
I create and make just to keep myself busy
It makes for a great and fantastical winning
At the end of every working of this phenomenon
It could boggle the mind if too long pondered on
I have drove myself insane in the attempt of it
In a literal sense that mental health is not exempt of it
I've learned to let go of this mysterious occurrence
That is the master of our world in every endurance
What else can be said about such strange activity
Is that the question has an answer beyond our longevity?
It can't be left alone as it is our sacred center
We are nothing without its movement and cannot be inventors
As it takes time to put together something new
Or lay out the structure of our discoveries and clues

While we may never escape the clutches of the cycle
I think it is fundamental to everything that's vital
We must accept the format in which existence is retained
Until we find some other law in which matter can be framed

The Lonely Walk

There is an anxiety that is caused by others
I have it every day and every night is to recover
I do not mean a paranoia that is unreal
I have made my assessment by how society deals
With the many types of personalities around
There is a constant demand to obey it's every sound
That the command of authority is not to be questioned
Not just a government but experts and professions
I look for a way to be left to be on my own
On a path that is to show how I was truly grown
Into what I am and have developed on the way
But not to prove I'm worthy of any others claim
To what they call good or healthy as a life
I want to clear resistance to me at any price
I am not to be told what to do and never have
I think it comes from what is inherently mad
That I have been born a personality of rage
From a source of power that lives beyond the grave
I do not claim to know all of what is true
All I claim to know is that I have to pay my dues
I did not begin to exist at my birth
I have lived in many ways and died away of hurt
I do not remember where I may have come
It is reasonable to me that somewhere I am from
I know I'm not alone in this rebellion of thought
And watch for any others who seek the lonely walk

What Is Faulted

It started in me as a way to conquer fear
To search deeper in the darkness of my fallen tears
I had lost all hope in the ways of life
And thought for the answer to change my mind
But the more I look the more I stayed
Among my own opinion that nothing will remain
In any sort of construct by deal to our thought
That heaven may be real, but she will have that lot
I understood that I am lost to such a fate
To reach for what is mine became my only game
As I saw no worth in worry or pain or grief
I am destined to a place that doesn't involve reprieve
This journey of mine took on a new relevance
I knew that something created all malevolence
That to be a creature is to be what is you
That what power created all made all imbued
Darkness is divine like the moon we see at night
To be able to see stars and the many hidden lights
I found inside this path a flame from another
That gave a different source of inside as a brother
The totality of galaxies dimmed by comparison
And my previous notions begin to feel embarrassing
At that point I could not believe in different knowledge
As the core of the teaching is what is real and what is faulted

It's Best Left Alone

I'm in a place where I feel that I'm not visible
In a sense that these people don't know more than miserable
They are lost in their heads mostly from their pain
Well, I have been there before I no longer and the same
I spent 13 years under the guidance of a counselor
As of this day which revealed to me my real color
I have had many errors in thought but not as a said
Usually from the experience of many rehabilitative beds
I noticed that I could not think more than one way
Meaning there were multitude of schisms in my brain
I have through this process of mapping out my mind
At least created a work. I'm of some kind
To utilize my knowledge, I've gained over the years
Thinking rather clearly now overcoming any fears
As of today, I am medicated and running smoothly
It was much needed from my youth being unruly
But now that I can function well to some degree
I noticed all too much that many cannot see
What I have done or what work I need to do
To maintain just sensible of normalcy to you
I don't say that these others don't also work hard
As I have no way of truly truly known of their cards
But I do say I am discredited by many of them
Not at all understood inside of the same fence
My mental illness has the full percentage of cause
Of this rift between the worlds these broken laws
I don't know if it may ever be patched together
I think it best left alone as it will not get better

Their Own Sort of Kingdom

I do not work for but work with a sinister kind
There are many names for the one that holds a bind
Onto me from the contract I have myself made
More with a understanding than for much to gain
I see that all people bind themselves into contract
The only difference is that they are a different match
They're working with other entities and energies
Then the one I chose to not call an enemy
As this partner has the reputation of an adversary
To most all other systems of burden to carry
As there is no system that holds to no weight
We must all do our part to reach our chosen fate
The same way we differ in people's and country
Is the same way we vary in the way we must see
The world we live in and how it revolves today
The foundation of verb begins all come from many take
It is only new that we embrace all forms of death
This was once a path that held peril in every step
Why is not known as I cannot see the origin
Of what is called evil that has always been grim
To me there is evil but not in what I do
Making two sides to the equation to be proved
Have many that I call enemy and unwanted
No less of a hierarchy exists in what is prompted
Everyone belongs to their own sort of kingdom
I remained in place and convey it as I see them

Unblocking The Mind

There is a tendency to overthink or overanalyze
Born of the need to complete the test to its size
It can be burdensome on me to have this compulsion
What may be called upon for a total immersion
I do not want to have this kind of character type
It is despairing to be held in its crib all night
I have mentioned this before to an audience unknown
And don't mean to repeat what has been already shown
But the purpose of my revelations are not to say
What is attractive or fantastic that I haven't relayed
I write what I do like a diarrhea that ventilates
My thought at the moment as it honestly correlates
To my current situation and mental perturbation
Not limited to any particular topic or relation
As I could be having issues with terrible griefs
Or lost an intellectual battle that is unseen
At the time of this clip into my focus of thought
I have found myself overwhelmed in what I have sought
And had a need to break down the intricate components
Of the process involved in myself made opponent
Effectively utilizing these skills and abilities
Of word plant and structure to delineate culpability
Because of the issue at hand is responsible
For the prompt creation of this matrix and tolerable
This is incredibly useful to me and understanding
What could be confounding me and by that demanding
What may not be deserved of its kind or ilk
Yet I cannot know until the ink is then spilled
Laying out the motive of a psychological hex
Unblocking the mind that was previously vexed

And I Am Left Alone

I think that there's a stigma placed upon me
Something attached to my reputation is taxing
What I work hard to attain and to develop
Like I have to pay for every word I spell up
For all that I am to simply live here and exist
Extracted from me from multiple antagonist
I admit too many wrongs that I don't care to list
I have been an adverse person too many I resist
But when I have the most innocent of intentions
I see certain people hold a grudge unmentioned
Like they are not humans too in another position
As if they somehow function with some other provision
I don't promote lawlessness in any of its forms
And don't inherently care what others do perform
Get that exact aspect of what makes me tick
Is what I see missing from the side of the strict
Ones that conform all too perfect and needless
But they suffer and lack in judgment to hear this
The make themselves blind what could be useful
From unexpected sources feeding wisdom by the spoonful
As this is not an easy life to have and survive
No matter how it started as have many been mine
So, while I may be annoyed at their criticizing looks
I don't care anymore than I would a fiction book
As the stigma only belongs to those that created it
And I'm left alone separate from those making it

How It Hurts to Pay this Price

These tattoos the completely cover my body
Have been taken from various forms of lodgings
I may not have been formally entered into one
Not including the exception that contact was done
Although the brother that I did help me along
Truly believed that I've seen the truth very strong
I don't think myself that I would be accepted
As the symbols I wear go on a different direction
I created many of them with a certain dark touch
As I don't believe that one side can hold much
There needs to be a balance of the different flames
Each needs a brotherhood to tend them everyday
I did not choose the lower path out of spite
I have seen I have a mind not belonging to the right
I understand fate and destiny and living times before
And saw a pattern in my ways to open up this door
I am what I am is a world of occult thought
That helped me to see I cannot change my lot
To argue I am different brings insanity to me
Only further proving I am darker than you see
My life does not belong to any other gate
I belong to a path that has seen many fates
I need not think that I know all the teachings
I do not believe that knowledge has all reachings
As it is useless without the ability to then do
What ignites the flame to open it for its use
A practical matter that is reserved for not many
And I don't recommend people try to that tending
The flame ignites the seeds inside of your mind
Both good and bad will start to grow from that vine

It is an excruciating pain for those fruits to grip
Then alone in a journey you can't afford to slip
After my experience I somehow brought forth
I find an independence from any other cohort
Although I would not shun to be given some advice
I need them to know how it hurts to pay this price

The Means Is Just a Medium

I don't pretend to be a moral or upstanding citizen
I have no true morals or laws that I have written
Not because it doesn't feel good to do what's right
But because the definition of right changes overnight
What was morally good a century ago or more
Is different than today by at least a hundred-fold
And I am not one to say where the future shall lead
Our people on this planet change with such frequency
Even today our morals are different in each nation
What is right to others also changes with each station
So, I question what is right in light of these variables
I am not to dictate what traits are better wearable
What decides my choice is what is practical today
How else can one choose with innumerable other ways?
I do not desire that I am held to great standards
Mostly from and need to maintain my mental manners
I might be defined as one who does not know
What is right or what is wrong as the judge did show
Making sense to these ideas that I find myself in
Not ever sure if what I do conforms to them
I know that I must at least have a blueprint
A concept of facts and trees that do bring
A sense of happiness and contentment and also success
If that is immoral than I have that at best
But even those goals and pursuits always change
In a progressive society of our educated brains
So, I remain flexible and how I obtained my ends
The means is just a medium that always tends to bend

How A Tangle Is Undone

Not wanting my statement to become at all diluted
I am unsure of when to pause and stop creating the music
I do hold back on some particular topics I have
As they are controversial in a way I can't move past
And I don't wish to offend any great number of people
That is not my purpose in this task I have agreed to
So, while I lay back and meditate on my real self
I think of what is unsaid that I might then tell
To the person who is interested in any kind of form
That propelled them to read on in my particular poems
I do not write them as only to communicate
I have spent a long time making them in a lonely state
That is largely my motive when laying down a sequence
I have a need to draw a straight line that will make sense
Out of the jungle of thoughts I've grow overtime
This is a form of navigation through the realm of my mind
In the end it is a give and take relationship
I see that I'm alone and am willing to be taking risk
To open myself up to a larger and greater venue
Of people that could possibly think the way I do
Or simply enjoy an interesting night of watching
How a tangle is undone from a terrible time of botching

The Worst of Life's Distortions

What makes love so difficult to maintain?
Why is it elusive or painful to our brains?
Of course, volumes of books may then be written
On just these two questions of emotional gripping
It is not only my problem but so many peoples
That even when I'm not many others are hurtful
It may not even be ours but still it affects us
Radiating its power in every other direction
The emotion is very hard to master and grasp
Not many survive it's all too inevitable crash
Sometimes not once, but many times over in life
That we are hurt or at least grieved by the strife
It cannot be avoided without turning in human
As it is an emotion that keeps our psychology moving
I'd say that we need to understand how it works
Because it can't be wished away or erased of its quirks
It must be inherent in the whole of our machine
Like blood and bone is essential to our every need
He must have a mechanic we have yet to discover
The fuse are body like a breath or dreaming slumber
All of our functions have turned out to be practical
His confusion may lie in our not being factual
That many get caught in imagining a fantasy
Without applying the mine to direct the dancing
Life calls for balance and all of its proportions
Without a happy love it is the worst of its distortions

Where My Focus Shall Remain

It's difficult to find others who care to know me
That care to understand why I am continuously going
But I don't let mistakes or faults to intrude
After years of them have happened in many multitudes
It's not that there don't exist people who care
It's my position and circumstance that distance the fair
Leaving me surrounded in an ocean of hateful misery
Caused from one thing or another doesn't matter to me
I just ate a fact of my life that has me abandoned
To an area the existence that is repeatedly remanded
I'll look for people who want to know me deeper
That don't care if the past or the media's reader
Those that will know that most reputations are fabricated
Or for the most part have true and much exaggerated
That it has been made from the focus mainly being
On the worst of the life of the person and meaning
I'm not saying that I have excuses for truths
I do say that I am not alone and that others do
Many different actions that could cause the ruin
Hidden in their mind and hopes it has no undoing
I don't care what others have down or even think
I do care not to be judge from people on the brink
Of what can even be called moderately presentable
I myself understand I am also most resentable
Making it all the more important to use compassion
In most all situations that have indeed for lasting
Companionship or friendship or family relations
Where my focus shall remain for the rest of my duration

A Perplexing Mystery

When I set a task for myself I'm compelled to finish it
In a manner that is obsessive and rarely diminishing
An energy or motive not regarding the length of time
It takes to complete and only then can I resign
Projects that take years and some over a decade
Controlling my life and all decisions that are made
It is productive to utilize this abundance of work
Is put towards a goal that doesn't actively hurt
My quality of life that I do in fact hold dear
I am only a man and don't expect myself to fear
Any part of myself that involves itself so much
Like this engine inside that refuses to reduct
A gravity of action that continues incessantly
From one object is to the next without it lessening
I know that an attempt to stop the vast production
Would end in a meltdown and my mental destruction
I let myself progress to what I inclined to naturally
Interested in the topics that combine and happening
I thought that maybe this could be very bad
But gave up that idea when discovering it is mad
To think that slothfulness is any way better
Has much more use in this ability's own measure
I leave this need to be creative and abundant
To its own design Lifting me into the encumbrance
It is strange to say that all this work is relaxing
A perplexing mystery that will never find me lacking

I Admit That It Is Right

Many nights I stare into the darkness of my room
Thoughts that will not stop as the day begins to bloom
At these times my heart will beat at a faster pace
Uncontrollable as it is, it is normal to my state
I have a condition that even professionals misunderstand
Classified as a disorder from an inherent genetic stamp
None of that matters to me as my body fails to function
I can't stand more than just hours of this without injunction
I need it to stop and slow down to then relax
Happens twice a day until it then comes back
I cannot proceed without some form of medical
Assistant that subsides the tides that were called
It is a subject that I have been very bitter about
Thinking that I should not have this need to shout
The symptoms remained after length of this struggle
I came to a resolution that I had to wear a muzzle
I am not okay without much of outside help
No matter the motive or perception of their shell
I don't want to think I am hopelessly incurable
But I don't have the luxury to hope for any miracle
I know that I suffer severely in this condition
And need to be balanced no matter how it's given
It came down to a decision of what is practical
To make it through my night text nothing magical
Science made a drug to stop the tearing psyche
I admit that it is right even with effects that might be
Damaging to the body in variously known ways
As long as my night gets over and I make it through the day

Of Its Own Mobility

I have a carefree forgetfulness about me
It's in stark contrast to the aspect that does see
On one hand I'm cursed repeat specific ideas
On the other I don't remember and I'm free as is
A blank page that has not been touched or written
Such as we find ourselves in this moment I'm smitten
It can be very helpful to be able to let go
Not a thought about my troubles am I let known
Until there comes the time that is a necessity
That I stir up and conjure and cook out a recipe
To bring forth what I desire as it will do
To remedy the situation, I currently fell into
It is somewhat practiced or rather encouraged
A positive note of my character I took to the edge
Maybe out of a need for survival of this place
Is there is far too much time to overthink and remake
Every little detail of every plan or possibility
Even of machinations that have no real plausibility
So, to lay back and forget or enjoy my day
Is it price of my personality I am much willing to pay?
I have one probability that could have contributed
I over-thought existence and how life is distributed
But there are laws at work that do the heavy lifting
All the calculations in this universe a drifting
Which left me with an unshaken and faithful stability
That whatever I do will happen then of its own mobility

Our Inevitable Questing

I am frequently told that I will never leave here
I don't believe in them or that my future is so clear
There have been hundreds of times I'd like to give up
That there is no point in the world does not miss us
Have lost this hope in the depths of my thought
Left alone in a medium that I had never sought
With no desire for a future or anything to feel
I contemplate the purpose of everything that's real
It became a habit to place myself inside of that
Other type of thought that takes away from what I have
It shows me that there is nothing at all in the end
But life nor death can provide what we portend
That to desire is a fatal motive always unfulfilled
Never satisfied as each one makes its own will
Within a multitude of warrants in every possible way
The direction of that one is always left a stray
While I may not agree with his are being abolished
I don't see what comes from what the people admonished
That without an active plan this creates a despair
As the one I face in this darkness that I stare
That no matter my agreement I have no argument
To what is made of fact about our envelopment
And investment in this world thought to be so big
It is made into a speck of dirt to be flicked
From the depths of Truth it is all put to question
What could be the answer of are in an inevitable questing?

A Vast Indenture

Sadness and depression have always played a part
In many instances of thought all the way from the start
The early stages of my psychology had a certain lack
The happiness that usually would be ingrained as a fact
But everybody possesses at least a substantial amount
This idea to me it was completely missing and was out
I did not know that I could change at all in mood
Leaving me to be a horrible example of my brood
The best I could laugh at only particular subjects
Which turned out to be by motive of malicious infects
My mind at a young age was incomprehensibly terrible
Not only bad inside but emotionally unbearable
At what was born in me that's so tour me asunder
When I began to learn that I was somehow wrong
It took a decade just to change and find where I belong
I have held on to a degree of that fatal sadness
It remains in my attitude that some perceive as madness
It is simply a solemnity towards the smaller things
Objects overlooked or the joy that topics bring
I may not smile as much as could be done
Get to force one out as detrimental to my fun
I speak to no one about my lost and lonely past
I don't think that I'm truly understood by this cast
I can't be relevant if I'm not relatable to them
I can't care at all if they can't listen to this pen
The moods of my life have become my story
Always as a background that never kept me boring
The emotions are a force I cannot at all control
In the sense that they will somehow pour out a roll
Of ripples in my daily meanderings and such

Parts of my routine and social interactive touch
I may be on my own in this particular venture
As even when its gone depression leaves a vast indenture

What I've Let Myself Become

I have one purpose in compiling any such book
As this one I work on in the cell of a crook
Is to contest the multiple rumors about me
Come with the stigma of conviction attaching
This becomes a vista of worlds opened up beyond
What is normally seen of me in any other prong
My true thoughts that have developed over years
Written down in a way that make me very clear
With this I think I can reach out to any
Who may be interested to what I am comprehending?
I don't see this as some way to cover up my faults
Those come with every page I scratch as I recall
The depths of my mind to the front center stage
My name then becomes what I have now untamed
It is not to say it is good or necessarily bad
All that is desired is the true self to be clad
Opening up connections to others on our planet
Let me have thoughts upon these Reflections I'm having
As I am very alone in this world of inner thought
Too many nights where I sit and stir the pot
Of my own studies that I've conjured in the past
Next with meditations on my psychological and cast
I don't have some benevolent or greatly divine intent
I just want to open up and let myself to vent
This is the being that I've let myself become
May be read by many or maybe not and only some

Misery Deplorable

I used to think that I once was somewhat smart
That I was better than most people from the start
Or understood subjects beyond the usual kind of scope
That without proper training I belonged within their rope
I can only say this detestable thought is the ego
What I came to understand is somehow living on its own
An ugly and putrid thing that digs its roots down deep
Into the personality of only certain susceptible human beings
I went through a process of destroying this monster
Although not intentionally I didn't let it conquer
After a particular experience I'd rather not recount
I was left humble and simply happy to live out
My daily life without any badgering anymore
From what can only be described as error to its core
Nothing from those days were of any worth
I'd rather be gone from our planet we call Earth
Now I see that I am rather ignorant of sorts
Of many things that I read that I did not know before
A newfound respect goes to those who pioneered
In all the many avenues and ventures far and near
Not only in our time but in events of history
That have left a lasting mark to near immortality
I don't expect to ever be that kind of remarkable
As I make my indentation that is hardly applaudable
The more I ponder on the greatest of intellectuals
The more I think I'd rather have humility protectable
If I ever find myself again arrogantly insufferable
I'll do my best to remember it causes misery deplorable

My Integrity

No longer plagued with such a low self-esteem
But I'm humbled by the mistakes I've had to redeem
My current predicament has been a long-fought battle
Of producing results that are seen as positively factual
Mainly for myself to prove I am a worthy person
That I have strong traits that really don't worsen
My quality of life that I've been told is not good
It has been those kinds of comments I battle and shout
I don't believe in my heart that I am inherently bad
So, when I hear to the contrary, I am malignantly sad
As I work so hard at bettering myself and vitality
I think I'm apart from what is the usual reality
I hold myself to a different standard in truth
As I have the time to explain myself to everyone
No one with dignity should ever work to have that done
But it continues incessantly that others do talk
And I continue to focus on deflecting their baulk
I have only so much energy allotted to me each day
That I need to put it towards the most productive way
It's not a unique problem that I state in these words
I hear of many people being badgered by the herds
It's not fun or amusing to have this kind of defense
And sad that our world is infected with this nonsense
I stopped being bitter or hateful about the topic
As that is also a waste of time not worthy to be opted
So, while the multitude at large talks a lot and gossips
I'll continue with my integrity as I know they have lost it

I Am Also Horrified

I didn't choose my religion out of personal ego
If I thought another was right that is where I would go
I declared very loud from the tattoos on my skin
But it is drowned out from other art that is akin
Like a person who wears a cross for fanciful jewelry
It's offending to a monk that then questions who he is
I have spent countless nights in perpetual suffrage
Plagued by my quest to balance out an average
Of truths to practical reality amongst the world
Not an easy task to interpret all the words
Of religion after a religion and to locate the one
Cut best suited my needs from where I had begun
I understand my choice turned out to be controversial
I think if I choose anything easy or Universal
I would not be in the one designed as this is
For people that are also in pain and anguish
I did not choose to be what I can only call tortured
So, I had to find something that explained what burned
I am cursed from some unknown past or deed
For being what I am and following some Creed
I do not believe in a handout to relieve me
No one else will pay the legs of an evil breed
As I do think it is a born and created gift
That has been persecuted and misunderstood as Sin
Happy our world today has more of a tolerance
I can be myself and belief and outward stance
But this path is not an easy way to be so glorified
It is hard to live with myself as I am also horrified

This Long Unending Journey

The retention and continuance of our basic consciousness
Is what I define as a sole in the mind's attentiveness
I really use the word as it seems to be misconstrued
To be involved in some sort of fantasy far misused
I think of it more in a relatable sort of concept
That without some structure we are doomed from the onset
I see some sort of need to have a mental storage unit
A function that's reliable and practical to use it
Something of energy itself has its own memory
And concentrates in two points for its own rendering
Of what works and what doesn't inside of this Realm
We may have pieces put together from various Helms
Remind maybe conglomerate of usable parts
That once upon a time had one of their own starts
In a sense that it will move to a body as we all did
Is there is no question that we hold intelligence
Made from some Source neither bad or benevolent
It seems to conform to the current predicament
At each new venue that it finds itself indicative
There's a long search for each of us to learn
Making it strange that a soul forgets at each turn
Where it came from and where it may be going
It not exactly lost in the flow of motion towing
As I move forward through this long unending journey
I know it is not over on the day I ride the gurney

The Sanctum of the Free

I see there is a separation of my mind to others
But the way I perceive, and think is all covered
There are many thoughts and opinions that I have
Yet when not spoken of they are completely passed
I use the opportunity as a form of concealment
As this world is full of people with much ill intent
I do not have to try hard to navigate this course
With others occupied inside of their own mental court
I become a Fascination to observe another mind
On that cannot understand to the point of being blind
All of this gives me a vast expanse of freedom
To enjoy my own interest and what I want done
This has not been some fear of being exposed
For a long once sought to explain to these foes
Everything that pertain to myself and every way
Only to come to this conclusion that I stay
There are far too many not in sync in my thought
But it is a waste of effort to try to change the lot.
I have currently one life to live that I need to place
Much to do in this relatively little time as man
It wants bothered me to see these others like this
Throwing away their energy and anger, bouts and fits
But I am not to blame for any other way of life
I have to cut the losses as is taught by all the wise
And everyone is included in what the few can see
Privately regarded as the sanctum of the free

This I Call My Prayer

I do not look for acceptance outside perspective
Of my mental process that I have long protected
I know I have a mental illness that infects me
Making it impossible to do any sort of self-dissecting
I need others to see and observe my inner thoughts
Just to make sure I alone am not self-taught
I should never be the one who teaches myself
I have no ability to measure what I dealt
I also need the much more positive of notes
But others can confirm what is described and wrote
Otherwise, I am left to compare myself to books
That are written about how the human is to look
Which is what I've done over all of these years
Faithful to these authors that I now hold so dear
As my life was essentially saved from their help
Of providing to the world their book upon the shelf
I cannot be more grateful to have had them there
My life would be otherwise full of pain and despair
This is the true world that I live in everyday
Holding myself to standards I have found along the way
In some manner of an unknown plethora of their gifts
I honestly don't know what to expect at this point
At this moment I'll be happy to finally make the joint
The connection to the world at large I don't believe will quit
This I called my prayer to anyone on that list

The Human Armory

I no longer claim to know so very much
I'm evolving in what my Essence does clutch
I once believed there was a choice in the matter
I now have an idea that birth is the master
That we can only choose to agree or disobey
What is predominantly motivating our way
A gravity of sorts moves our soul and being
From a source that is not all theory and meaning
Is material at its core and limits our reach
Not positive or negative but unique in each
This material Force changes and constructs us
To be like it over the years it hugs us
We may then move on to another material hub
Only to be morphed into the shape of that one
It is futile and quite miserable to think not
As that creates schism with each left to rot
The body and the mind are one entity together
May be separate from before but now need to be tethered
It is essential to remember or learn of their roots
To make sure that the vessel can grow new shoots
Move forward through life and what lies beyond
Which is determined from the change in the song
Of the energy that makes our essence and harmony
Singing through the eons of the human armory

The Discretion of My Deeds

To express myself in this written form
Is beyond the scope of any usual norm
I do not do this as some popular social mode
Of thought that has taken our world by storm
The revelation came to me at night when alone
After reflecting on someone complimenting my poem
That I am not what others see when I recite
The words onto canvas from the depths of my mind
That this is in fact a different and separate section
Of my brain that collects and reflects its own perception
It takes effort and energy not usually available
To any part of my mind that is normally detailable
That my psychology is parallel to others that I use
That my mind is writing down from an angle not in view
I read in occult philosophy and theology
That this kind of action is the real personality
That the world and all its current material constructs
Are taken away when we create a written mantra
The section of our soul that bleeds out every line
Is the part of ourself that exists outside of time
It is not unique to me in any particular way
As many people do it in various forms today
I am just comfortable in utilizing it like this
And think i relieve a pressure that has me in its grip
That if I don't let it go and flow out its every need
I'll be somehow abusing the discretion of my deeds
I may not have one life, I may have many others
But today, I put to use what I see cannot be smothered

All that I Am

I am taking a risk at being this blatantly candid
It is social suicide to place these words at markets stamping
I do not seek pity in that seemingly simple statement
I am just again seeking to describe what I'm facing
In daily life here and in any way connected to it
I do not care what others think as I continue to do this
I have found that I must seek a larger audience
To have people that are like me or at least applauding
A heartfelt and genuine approach to a field of art
It may not be expert but it entertains the part
I am not looking for any fluffed up recognition
Just anyone who likes these ideas and particular rendition
Of an experience that has taken me to this place
At length I explain in my own individual taste
I don't know what started me with these pens
Long ago I wrote and saw something in my vents
That was very much different than normal descriptions
I had a bend towards occult philosophical inscription
I did not intend it and noticed it to be subconscious
As I wrote out the words it was depth that I wanted
It became my own choice of writing to pursue
That I probably would not write a book without tune
That is my reasoning in making myself sacrifice
My immediate outward existence that is a mask in life
I am the type of person to jump into the deep end
Not without concern but with the goal I intend
I allow myself to be all that I am in this page
Because if I don't I have no freedom from this cage

That Abominable Sin

I want to express my thoughts about my mother's family
Without saying too much of the predicament I'm managing
I try to convince myself that I have no need to suffer
Yet I feel an insurmountable amount of grief that is clustered
Into knots of emotion that clog my psychological will
I need to overcome this everyday even after a decade still
It is not about me that I relay these descriptions for
They are caused from my concern of their welfare and core
The seed and spark of life's motivation that they need
To continue daily tasks without hindrance to proceed
And pursue what they value and have left to protect
I am worried I am a burden even inside of this fence
That somehow, I weigh down their conscience and vitality
That I am a drag of a memory that battles the free
I do not desire this and have no outlet to stop it
If someone cannot let go of the past or drop it
I cannot do that for them in the way that is needed
For them to heal the wounds so importantly heeded
I have done what I can for myself in this place
Utilizing tools and access to assistance that I craved
Doing any sort of reconstruction of my mentality
Was not an option to do alone as it is all too rattling
And that is the depth of my fear for my brood
That they are not dissolving that wall as is shrewd
As that is the most unhealthy non-action to take
Left alone these psychological damages will break
Even more of their lines that have already been taxed
By some unfortunate event not logical with facts
I am the cause to the greater degree of the situation
But how do I remedy something out of reach of my graduation?
It is a bad set of circumstances I find myself in
As I am not able to undo that abominable sin

How The Bones May Fall

There is an uncontrollable force that propels me
I cannot say exactly what this does mean
Day and night I'm on a path that is unknown
I have no choice at all but to just let go
I have found through time that this is unusual
It is something different than the steps that you would go
This force has a feeling of rage behind it
Like an entity that has me caged inside it
For years I thought that I was simply horrible
Then noticed a difference between me and this horror show
That I am not what this body and life are
And have tried to stop and heal all of my scars
Yet even in the calmest and happiest moments
I still see and watch from a distance the coldest
Nothing truly describes what it is outside
A contrast of white to the black of my mind
The only solace and content that I do have
Is knowing the explanation of what is seen as man
What propels me forward is an ancient call
And I am forced to obey how the bones may fall

My Future on the Brink

I have been a certain way all of my life
At first very ill with the plague of pride
I had a self-centered ego that would not quit
And an arrogance of anger that spoke from my lips
I have been made a fool out of my own faults
With no one to blame I could never stand tall
For a while I made excuses that I needed to be
What I was to others who never did agree
I made a self-hate inside my mind
That was not hidden but conscious all the time
As I did have regrets and remorse of what I did
And could not believe I was the worst of all the kids
After years of contemplation, I had begun to find
New ways of thought to put me on a different line
Not to impress anyone as they are not around
I found a need to be happy for just myself
To make sure that I liked the solitude I felt
To be silent and alone yet content in what I do
It became the foremost of my character's use
That I use my body and mind and personality
To reach beyond my limit with dynamic versatility
I am in a space today that I can no longer relate
To that boy that I was so damaged in the brain
Today, I speak with a voice I have unparalleled
From any other moment of time in life's carousel
Of my revolving doors that change the way I think
The past forever gone and my future on the brink

To Clear My Mind

I do not work at all to impress anyone around me
Or anyone in general that could possibly have known me
It does not come from a carelessness of presentability
It is an experience I've had that creates a resentability
That I don't need approval from people who cannot prove
What they themselves are worth in an area they choose
It is a problem faced by lots of individual minds
That there is an incessant encroaching upon their kind
By what can only be described as a decision to be lethargic
It is difficult for me to overlook that sort of margin
I don't believe that this vast amount can be disabled
Not in any medical sense that they can then be labeled
I do understand a true mental illness or problem
But even that can be mitigated with self-help solving
Even amongst certain active groups of the community
They are also infected with this disease of talkativity
Gossip and nonsense rather than focus and work
I do my best to not be bitter and them I do ignore
And I also understand that my view may be jaded
From my circumstance of close quarters that's created
By the system that I'm in that puts me so near
To these kinds of people that don't have a plan so clear
It has created on myself a tough skin and exterior
That protects myself within that I do not weaken wearier
It can be taxing to go through at the worst of times
I don't expect it to get better as I sigh and clear my mind

A Burdened World

I look into her eyes and see apparent awareness
And think to myself that I shouldn't be careless
I'm in a dream but what I see are all people
Starting at me while I lay in the fetal
I'm not adverse to the idea of a real world
That revolves around the souls of those sleep curled
Entities that take on the shape of humans
And watch the thoughts of each man and woman
Many believe we enter into the astral plane
When we lay down at night and stop our brains
The more I see the eyes of these creatures
The more I believe they have true features
Not bodies with blood that pump in their veins
They are dead to us with no life to claim
Not the kind of life that we usually have
But they do have something still within grasp
Something that holds them exactly as they are
Staring with a gaze that does become their mark
It is unknown who or what that we see
When we enter into this otherworldly dream
Anything could happen every time that I do
But it's the same every time I encounter and view
The look of what is unmistakably real
A conscious being or entity with eyes of steel
And the strangest of all is they never say a word
Just staring at me with a look of a burdened world

A World Without Psychosis

I don't believe in what certain people say
I think my soul has a heavy price to pay
What is usually called mental illness and distortion
Could be any number of causes in effected proportions
A life that recurs in the same place on the planet
Could be back again to create the same damage
Or a contract may have been made before the birth
And the body that is entered is the vessel to work
I have yet to figure what my fate is exactly
As I have yet to see what my past was mapping
I once thought I had begun here completely new
Just a being with a different and peculiar view
But have since then added together a few ideas
That have been garnished from sources of many arenas
There is in fact one solid structure to truth
That is based on material reality unmoved
Regardless of places another dimension may have
We cannot have time not on a rigid path
To realize that some sort of compass was created
Is also to see that no direction is vacated
Whatever it is that severely plagues my soul
I know was set in motion by these various goal
So, while the psychologist speaks again a diagnosis
I drift off in thought to a world without psychosis

As My Case Is Laid to Bed

I do my best not to be biased against the government
To understand that there was a process law underwent
I understand that there are different people at large
That society is made up of a variety all in charge
Of all facets and aspects of what's needed to sustain
A community and country like one working brain
It is not their fault that I am in this position
Where I am at the mercy of the law and disposition
Of its interpreter that shall make my future known
To the public that was the victim to this rogue
I do not make excuses any longer about this crime
I am responsible for what happened at the time
I do claim that there is a right way to approach
The specific circumstances that I in fact stoked
Which is the middle ground to this courtroom drama
I need to stand tall to the state and their mantra
That all crime is severe and needs a vast punishment
I need to understand that there are levels of admonishment
To not give in to what seems to be intimidation
That I don't deserve a life without trepidation
I did do wrong but also have other human needs
That belong side by side in this argument of creeds
I don't know what may come in this long battle
Of court upon court of decisions to be handled
One day I will have a final answer to be said
And need to make peace as my case is laid to bed

About The Author

Roger Teas was found legally insane under Alaska's verdict of guilty but mentally ill for murders he did not intend to commit. He sought answers for the discrepancies in the field of psychology through philosophy and religion. These poems are a brief glimpse of what he has found.

Born as Jason Abbott in Sitka, Alaska, and being incarcerated at the immediate adult age of 18, he thinks that there has been no other source of information about himself or his reputation besides what has been provided through the media of his crime. While not intended to paint a perfect picture, the words of these poems are meant to shed light on the other aspects of his personality.

Roger Teas has studied philosophy and practiced occult religions for over a decade before the publishing of these poems, and has periodically wrote poetry throughout that time. He has no official certificates or degrees in art, but does not limit himself from the possibility. At the moment, he believes the freedom of expression is the greatest liberty of all.

www.ingramcontent.com/pod-product-compliance
Lightning Source LLC
Chambersburg PA
CBHW071917070526
44583CB00016B/2028